Roseland
Bon journée ♡
Bon voyage

avec amie
J. Kem
6/02

Rendez-vous with
FRANCE
à la Jill Butler

The
Globe
Pequot
Press

Guilford, Connecticut

Text and illustrations: Jill Butler
Design: Jill Butler
Pronunciations: FrenchSounds, LLC

Library of Congress Cataloging-in-Publication Data
Butler, Jill
Rendez-vous with France / Jill Butler.
p. cm.
Includes index.
ISBN 0-7627-2211-8
1. France—Guidebooks.

DC16.B87 2001
448.3'421—dc21   2001040828

Manufactured in Korea
First Edition/First Printing

Introduction

Getting ready to go to a foreign country can be daunting. For me it's a mixed bag of excitement and nervousness. How will I find my way? Will I have the courage to walk into a restaurant, order something, and actually know what it is . . . before it's placed in front of me? Where will I find what I need? Will there be friendly people to help me?

France has a reputation—you know the one—about not being particularly friendly (fortunately that's rapidly changing). Some French speak English, but not all.

 Point and Pronounce was created to lower the anxiety and raise the comfort level. It came as an inspiration based quite simply on my own desperation! When first living in France 15 years ago, I kept thinking, "If only I knew what 'it' looked like then maybe I could find it." The "it" was everything from a mailbox (p. 124) to a taxi stand (p. 5). Thus was born this visual guide.

Pointing may not be pretty, but it can be useful and may well get you what you desperately need. Making the effort to pronounce "it" can demonstrate your willingness to try and hopefully will engage or amuse the one you've chosen to assist you on your search. Be sure to check out the tips on asking for help on page 21 as well as some restaurant etiquette on page 32.

This is my gift to you of what I've learned both visually and experientially while finding my way around France.

Don't be afraid to write in your book. I've purposely put in pages for notes and addresses to remember. I'd love to hear about your experiences using this book, so feel free to leave me a message on my Web site, **www.jillbutler.com.** I'll do my best to respond to your questions and/or suggestions.

Bon Voyage, and above all, keep your sense of humor at all times!

Jill Butler

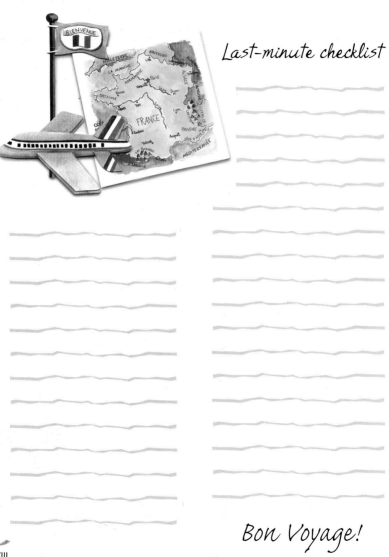

Last-minute checklist

Bon Voyage!

Traveling

En Voyage

L'Arrivée

l'avion
lah•vee•yohn

les aéroports
layz ah•ehr•oh•pohr

Make sure you know which airport you are arriving at or leaving from.

le drapeau français
luh drah•poh frahn•seh

la carte de débarquement
lah kahrt duh day•bahr•kuh•mahn

l'immigration
lee•mee•grahs•yohn

le passeport
luh pahs•por

2

Les Bagages

LIVRAISON des BAGAGES
lee•vreh•zohn day bah•gahj

OBJETS à DÉCLARER

DOUANE

la douane
lah doo•wah•nuh

Les euros started to circulate on January 1, 2002 (see p. 121).

un chariot
uhn shah•ree•oh

BUREAU de CHANGE

US $: EUR
YEN: EUR

bureau de change
boo•roh duh shahnj

SORTIE/EXIT

BUS   TAXI

sortie
sohr•tee

3

Les Transports

la location de voitures
lah luh•kahs•yohn duh vwah•toor

un permis international
uhn pehr•mee
ehn•tehr•nahs•yuh•nahl

Renting a car with a standard shift is less expensive than an automatic. It's much cheaper to book well in advance from the U.S.

An international driver's license is suggested for stays over 3 months.

le chauffeur
luh shoh•fuhr

une limousine
oon lee•moo•zeen

le bus
luh boos

un bus: public bus
un car: tourist bus

une valise
oon vah•leez

un taxi
uhn tahk•see

une tête de station
oon teht duh stahs•yohn

TAXI !

This will get you
nowhere.

Find a taxi station,
une tête de station,
and wait patiently.

You can also call
for a taxi.

Les Taxis:
Taxis accept credit cards
when displayed. There
may be a minimum
amount.

Tips are included in the
fare (a few extra coins are
always appreciated). A per
bag charge will be added.

Beware! Fares are double
all day Sunday and
evenings after 7 p.m.

Les Trains

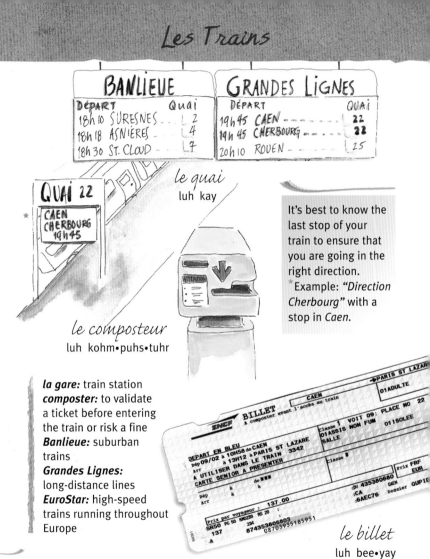

BANLIEUE

DÉPART		Quai
18h10	SURESNES	2
18h18	ASNIÈRES	4
18h30	ST. CLOUD	7

GRANDES LIGNES

DÉPART		QUAI
19h45	CAEN	22
19h45	CHERBOURG	22
20h10	ROUEN	25

QUAI 22

CAEN
CHERBOURG
19h45

le quai
luh kay

le composteur
luh kohm•puhs•tuhr

It's best to know the last stop of your train to ensure that you are going in the right direction.
Example: "Direction Cherbourg" with a stop in *Caen*.

la gare: train station
composter: to validate a ticket before entering the train or risk a fine
Banlieue: suburban trains
Grandes Lignes: long-distance lines
EuroStar: high-speed trains running throughout Europe

le billet
luh bee•yay

6

For tickets or reservations, you'll need to know:

la date de départ: day of departure
lah daht duh day•pahr

l'heure de départ: time of departure
luhr duh day•pahr

la date de retour: return date
lah daht duh ruh toor

l'heure de retour: time of return
luhr duh ruh toor

aller simple: one way
ah•lay sehm•pluh

aller-retour: round-trip
ah•lay ruh•toor

première classe: first class
pruhm•yehr klahs

deuxième classe: second class
duhz•yehm klahs

place réservée: reserved seat
plahs ray•zehr•vay

fumeur: smoking
foo•muhr

non-fumeur: nonsmoking
nohn foo•muhr

wagon-lit: sleeping car
vah•gohn lee

le train
leh trehn

Hotels to return to

Other accommodation choices:

une auberge: inn

une auberge de jeunesse: youth hostel

un B et B: bed-and-breakfast

une chambre: a room in private home or hotel

une chambre complète: a room with breakfast

un gîte rural: a private farm or home welcoming travelers

une pension complète: a room with 3 meals

une demi-pension: a room with breakfast and 1 other meal

Room availability:

disponible: available

complet: full

L'Hôtel

l'hôtel
loh•tehl

le bagagiste
luh bah•gah•jeest

la clé
lah klay

RÉCEPTION
ray•sehp•see•yohn

CONCIERGE
kohn•see•yehrj

9

La Chambre

lah shahm•bruh

le placard
luh plah•kahr

une commode
oon kuh•muhd

une lampe
oon lahm•puh

le bureau
luh boo•roh

un lit pour une personne
uhn lee poor oon pehr•suhn

Check your room before accepting it! Ask to see other choices if you're not happy.

un oreiller
uhn uh•ray•yay

un grand lit pour deux personnes
uhn grahn lee poor duh pehr•suh•nuh

une ampoule
oon ahm•pool

une couverture
oon koo•vehr•toor

un lit supplémentaire
uhn lee soo•play•mahn•tehr

la climatisation
lah klee•mah•tee•zahs•yohn

un réveil
uhn ray•vay•yuh

la télévision
lah tay•lay•veez•yohn

un magnétoscope
uhn mahn•yeh•tuhs•kuhp

un téléphone
uhn tay•lay•fuh•nuh

un coffre-fort
uhn kuh•fruh fohr

le chauffage
luh shoh•fahj

un ventilateur
uhn vahn•tee•lah•tuhr

11

La Salle De Bains

lah sahl duh behn

le lavabo
luh lah•vah•boh

l'eau froide
loh frwah•duh

l'eau chaude
loh shoh•duh

une baignoire
oon behn•wahr

un gant de toilette
uhn gahn duh twah•leht

une serviette
oon sehr•vee•yeht

les toilettes
lay twah•leht

le bidet
luh bee•day

une douche
oon doosh

12

une brosse à dents
oon bruhs ah dahn

un rasoir
uhn rah•zwahr

le dentifrice
luh dahn•tee•frees

la mousse à raser
lah moos ah rah-zay

un peignoir
uhn pehn•wahr

le savon
luh sah•vohn

le shampooing
luh shahm•pwehn

le papier toilette
luh pahp•yay twah•leht

les Kleenex
lay klee•nehks

13

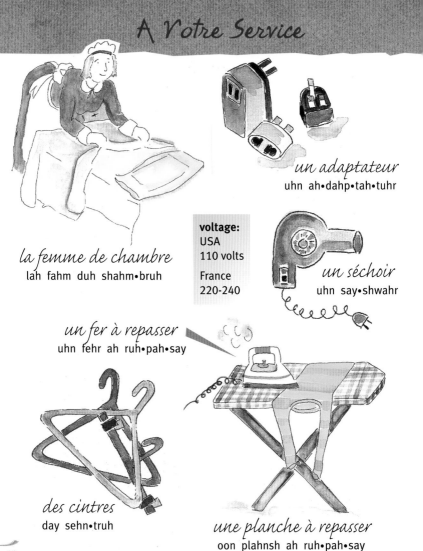

la femme de chambre
lah fahm duh shahm•bruh

un adaptateur
uhn ah•dahp•tah•tuhr

voltage:
USA
110 volts

France
220-240

un séchoir
uhn say•shwahr

un fer à repasser
uhn fehr ah ruh•pah•say

des cintres
day sehn•truh

une planche à repasser
oon plahnsh ah ruh•pah•say

un petit déjeuner complet
uhn puh•tee day•juh•nay kohm•pleh

une cafetière
oon kah•fuht•yehr

un verre
uhn vehr

une bouteille d'eau
oon boo•teh•yuh doh

le service en chambre
luh sehr•vees ahn shahm•bruh

les glaçons
lay glah•sohn

la salle à manger
lah sahl ah mahn•jay

15

Sightseeing

un musée:
museum

une cathédrale:
cathedral

une église:
church

un château:
castle

un manoir: large
country house

une maison:
house

La Tour Eiffel
lah toor eh•fehl

Métro: Branly/Trocadero

16

Paris

Le Moulin Rouge
luh moo•lehn rooj

Métro: Pigalle

Le Sacré-Coeur
luh sah•kray•kuhr

L'Arc de Triomphe
lahrk duh tree•yohmf

Métro: Etoile

Avenue des Champs-Elysées
ah•vuh•noo day shahn•zay•lee•zay

Le Louvre
luh loo•vruh

Métro: Louvre

La Place de la Concorde
lah plahs duh lah kohn•kohrd

Métro: Concorde

Notre-Dame
nuh•truh•dahm

Métro: Hôtel de Ville

Le Centre Pompidou
luh sahn•truh pohm•pee•doo

17

Les Directions

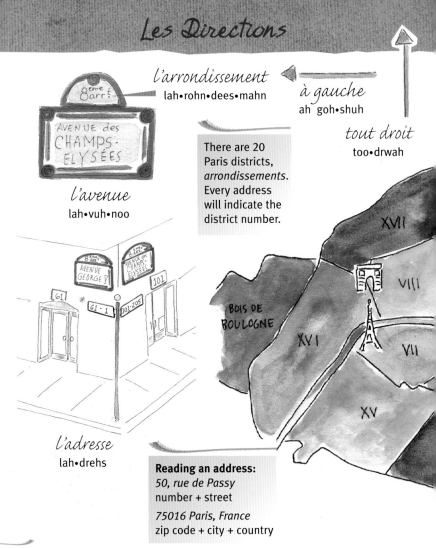

l'arrondissement
lah•rohn•dees•mahn

à gauche
ah goh•shuh

tout droit
too•drwah

AVENUE des CHAMPS-ELYSÉES

l'avenue
lah•vuh•noo

There are 20 Paris districts, *arrondissements*. Every address will indicate the district number.

AVENUE GEORGE V

AVENUE des CHAMPS-ELYSÉES

XVII

BOIS DE BOULOGNE

VIII

XVI

XV

VII

l'adresse
lah•drehs

Reading an address:
50, rue de Passy
number + street

75016 Paris, France
zip code + city + country

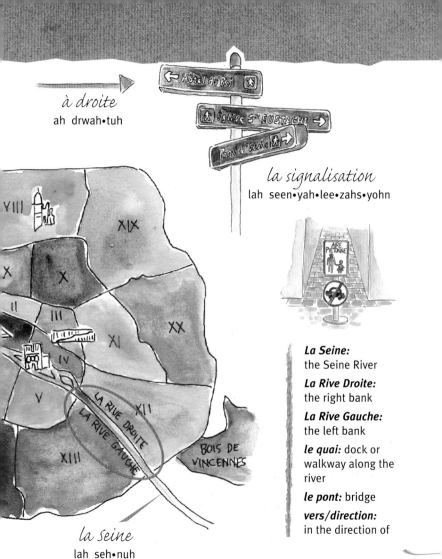

à droite
ah drwah•tuh

la signalisation
lah seen•yah•lee•zahs•yohn

La Seine:
the Seine River

La Rive Droite:
the right bank

La Rive Gauche:
the left bank

le quai: dock or
walkway along the
river

le pont: bridge

vers/direction:
in the direction of

la Seine
lah seh•nuh

19

A Pied   En Vélo

Piétons

à pied
ah pee•yay

As a pedestrian, you are supposed to have the right-of-way, but *faites attention!*

Les rollers skate with a police escort every Friday at 10 p.m. from the *Place d'Italie, Paris*

en rollers
ahn roh•lehr

en vélo
ahn vay•loh

En Métro

Asking for directions

When stopping someone on the street, always excuse yourself for bothering them.

If speaking in English, speak slowly, enunciate, and do not shout if they do not understand. They are not required to speak your language.

To get help and to be understood is the goal. Point to something in this book, spell the word (p. 150), or try charades.

A generous *merci beaucoup* is imperative!

"merci beaucoup, monsieur/madame"
mehr•see boh•koo
muhs•yuh /
mah•dahm

Le Métro

le métro
luh may•troh

la bouche de métro
lah boosh duh may•troh

le guichet
luh ghee•shay

un ticket
uhn tee•kay

une carte orange
oon kahrt uh•rahnj

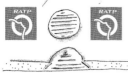

un carnet
uhn kahr•nay

Purchase tickets in
métro, autobus, or
a *tabac* (p. 127).

un ticket: one trip,
métro or bus

un carnet:
10 tickets

carte orange:
unlimited trips,
métro or bus, for
one month

Le Bus

le composteur (métro)
luh kohn•puhs•tuhr (may•troh)

le composteur (bus)
luh kohn•puhs•tuhr (boos)

les itinéraires
layz ee•tee•nay•rehr

le train
luh trehn

l'autobus
loh•toh•boos

la station
lah stahs•yohn

> You must validate your ticket or risk a fine. Keep your ticket; it's sometimes needed to exit.
>
> *Métro* tickets are used for the *métro* and bus. Good maps are inside both.

23

En Voiture

ahn vwah•toor

2 voies/ **90** = **56** MPH
duh vwah

4 voies/ **110** = **68** MPH
kah•truh vwah

Be alert! Motorcycles, *les motos*, create their own traffic lane, *voie*, where one doesn't exist.

une moto
oon moh•toh

1 kilomètre = 0.6 mile
uhn kee•luh•meh•truh

l'huile
lweel

4 litres = 1 US gallon
kah•truh lee•truh

L'Autoroute

l'autoroute à 6 voies/
loh•toh•root ah see vwah

STATION-SERVICE

Gagnez
les
Points
chez
Total

Café
Sandwiches
chocolat

TOILETTES

DAME   HO

Les Services
café
toilettes
jouets
presse
garage

oon stahs•yohn sehr•vees

un poste d'essence
uhn puhst deh•sahns

l'essence
leh•sahns

PREPAREZ
9ᵀ

le péage
luh pay•yaj

Toll booths, *les péages,* accept credit cards.

The cheapest gas, *l' essence,* can be bought at a *centre commercial* (p. 99).

sans plomb: no lead

super SP: super unleaded

gazole: diesel

25

une dépanneuse
oon day•pah•nuhz

les feux
lay fuh

un pneu
uhn pnuh

un pneu crevé
uhn pnuh kruh•vay

"au secours" (S.O.S.)
oh suh•koor

un parcmètre
uhn pahrk•meh•truh

un mécanicien
uhn may•kah•nees•yehn

l'eau
loh

une batterie
oon bah•tree

Centre Ville

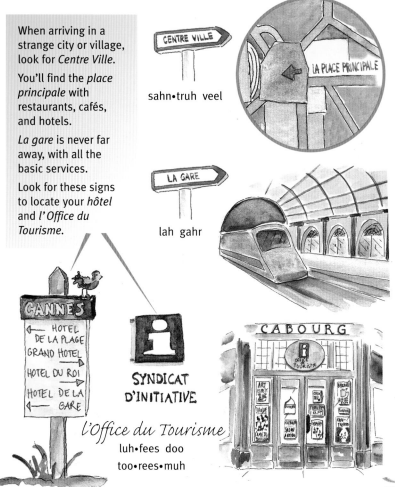

When arriving in a strange city or village, look for *Centre Ville*.

You'll find the *place principale* with restaurants, cafés, and hotels.

La gare is never far away, with all the basic services.

Look for these signs to locate your *hôtel* and *l'Office du Tourisme*.

CENTRE VILLE

LA PLACE PRINCIPALE

sahn•truh veel

LA GARE

lah gahr

CANNES
HOTEL DE LA PLAGE
GRAND HOTEL
HOTEL DU ROI
HOTEL DE LA GARE

SYNDICAT D'INITIATIVE

l'Office du Tourisme
luh•fees doo
too•rees•muh

CABOURG

A La Campagne

LA MER
lah mare

LE PHARE
luh fahr

LA PLAGE
lah plahj

LE PORT
luh pohr

la chapelle
lah shah•pehl

LE PONT
luh pohn

la rivière
lah reev•yehr

LA FORÊT

lah foh•ray

LE VIGNOBLE

luh veen•yuh•bluh

PIQUE-NIQUE

peek•neek

CIRCUIT TOURISTIQUE

The best views can be found by following *les circuits touristiques,* the green roads, marked on any Michelin road map.

LE LAC

luh lahk

LE CAMPING

luh kahm•peeng

... villages to remember

... forever in search of the perfect
stone cottage

Le Départ

les billets
lay bee•yay

le porteur
luh pohr•tuhr

Le départ: departure

It's time to say *"au revoir."*

It's a good idea to reconfirm your flight.

As you set off for the airport,
double check that you're headed
to the correct one.

At the airports and train stations, *les
porteurs* are rare! *Les chariots* or carts
are more abundant . . . and free. They're
found at the entrance, *la porte d'entrée,*
or go inside and look for one.

Remember to pass by the *détaxe* (p. 92)
desk **before** checking in. They may not
check your purchases, but they will ask
if you have them with you. And the
answer needs to be *"oui, monsieur."*

Great places to return to

au restaurant

You can always tell the Americans have arrived. Yes, we are noisy, boisterous, and hilarious. **Take a minute to listen and adjust to the restaurant's noise level.**

Getting the waiter's attention: Snapping your fingers is not a choice; neither is *"Garçon."*

"Monsieur or Mademoiselle, s'il vous plaît" is preferred.

Cafés et Restaurants

Les Restaurants

un café-restaurant
uhn kah•fay rehs•toh•rahn

une brasserie
oon brahs•ree

un bistrot
uhn bees•troh

un bar à vin
uhn bahr•ah•vehn

un grand restaurant
uhn grahn rehs•toh•rahn

une brasserie: a brewery by origin; German-inspired foods as well as seafood, *les fruits de mer*. Noisy, large, friendly. Serves late into the morning, open Sunday evenings.

un café-restaurant: reasonable food at reasonable prices. Good for break-fast, lunch, dinner. Don't expect a nonsmoking section.

un bistrot: small, cozy, family-style food and atmosphere. "Bistro" is the English spelling.

un "grand" restaurant: the chef is often the owner; the more discreet the exterior, the higher the prices.

un bar à vin: friendly, noisy ambience, good food, lots of wine to taste.

Salon De Thé   Crêperie

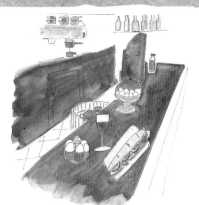

un végétarien
uhn veh•jeh•tari•yehn

un café au comptoir
uhn kah•fay oh kohn•twahr

Lots of choices for simple dining:

un self-service: cafeteria

un traiteur: catering and delicious take-out,
à emporter

au comptoir: a simple, quick lunch at the counter

un salon de thé:
simple good food served in a tearoom environment

une crêperie: a kiosk selling crêpes "to go"

un végétarien: a chance to experience the freshness of French vegetables

une crêperie
oon kreh•pree

Traiteur

Salon de Thé
sal•lohn duh tay

un self-service
uhn self•sehr•vees

Les PLATS
Tie de Veau
de BOEUF

Salades • SANDWICHES
carottes pommes de
celeri
chef

TRAITEUR à
EMPORTER

Pierre
TRAITEUR

le traiteur
luh treh•tuhr

LES RESTAURANTS
SERVI

PETIT DÉJEUNER
à
7h - 10h30

DÉJEUNER
à
midi - 14h

DÎNER
à
19h30 - 21h30

SOUPER
à
20h   2h
APRES THÉÂTRE

LES CAFÉS
à
7h - 21h

h = the hour of

37

Les Personnages

le voiturier
luh vwah•toor•yay

le maître d'hôtel
luh meh•truh doh•tehl

la voiture
lah vwah•toor

le vestiaire
luh vehs•tee•yehr

le serveur
"Monsieur"
luh sehr•vuhr

la serveuse
"Mademoiselle"
lah sehr•vuhz

38

le barman
luh bahr•mahn

le chef
luh shehf

le sommelier
luh suh•muhl•yay

Don't be surprised to see a dog or a cat in the restaurant . . . but forget about a doggie bag.

39

A Table

une chaise
oon shehz

une table
oon tah•bluh

When entering a restaurant you will be asked *"combien de couverts?"*: "how many place settings?" (i.e. how many people?)

un couvert
uhn koo•vehr

un verre à vin
uhn vehr ah vehn

une tasse
oon tahs

une carafe
oon kah•rahf

un verre d'eau
uhn vehr doh

a. **une serviette**
oon sehr•vee•yeht

b. **une fourchette**
oon foor•sheht

c. **une assiette**
oon ahs•yeht

d. **un couteau**
uhn koo•toh

e. **une cuillère**
oon kwee•yehr

a.
b.
c.
d.
e.

40

carte
kahrt

le menu
luh muh•noo

le service: tipping
A tip of 15%
plus a tax of
20.6% is **almost
always*** included.
You need not
leave anything
additional. If the
service was
exceptional, a
few extra coins
are always
appreciated.

le plat du jour
luh plah doo joor

la carte:
the menu

le menu: set choices
at a fixed price, some-
times includes wine,
usually not coffee.
May not include the tip.

***service non compris
(s.n.c.):**
service not included

à la carte:
every dish priced
individually

plat du jour: chef's
special of the day

Recipes discovered

...en Provence,
it's the garlic and
tomatoes that I love

La Cuisine Française
food as art

Les Fruits

les pêches
lay pehsh

les figues
lay fee•guh

les pruneaux
lay proo•noh

la prune
lah proon

Great ingredients make great cuisine.

le raisin
luh reh•zehn

un melon
uhn muh•lohn

un avocat
uhn ah•voh•kah

les abricots
layz ah•bree•koh

l'ananas
lah•nah•nah

les oranges
layz uh•rahnj

les citrons verts
lay see•trohn vehr

les bananes
lay bah•nah•nuh

le citron
luh see•trohn

la noix de coco
lah nwah duh koh•koh

les poires
lay pwahr

le pamplemousse
luh pahm•pluh•moos

les mandarines
lay mahn•dah•reen

la pomme
lah puh•muh

Les Fruits

les mûres
lay moor

les cerises
lay suh•reez

les airelles
layz eh•rehl

les cassis
lay kah•see

les groseilles
lay groh•zeh•yuh

les framboises
lay frahm•bwahz

les marrons
lay mah•rohn

les fraises
lay frehz

les noisettes
lay nwah•zeht

les amandes
layz ah•mahn•duh

les noix
lay nwah

Les Légumes

les carottes
lay kah•ruht

les haricots verts
lay ah•ree•koh•vehr

le maïs
luh mah•ees

l'oseille
loh•zeh•yuh

les primeurs: the earliest young vegetables— a real delicacy

le chou
luh shoo

les petits pois
lay puh•tee pwah

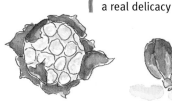

le chou-fleur
luh shoo fluhr

les choux de Bruxelles
lay shoo duh broo•sehl

les flageolets
lay flah•juh•lay

Les Légumes

un artichaut
uhn ahr•tee•shoh

les asperges
layz ahs•pehrj

le fenouil
luh fuh•noo•yuh

les betteraves
lay beh•trahv

les endives
layz ahn•deev

le cresson
luh kreh•sohn

les poireaux
lay pwah•roh

la laitue
lah leh•too

le radis
luh rah•dee

les pommes de terre
lay puhm duh tehr

les tomates
lay tuh•maht

les épinards
layz ay•pee•nahr

les citrouilles
lay see•troo•yuh

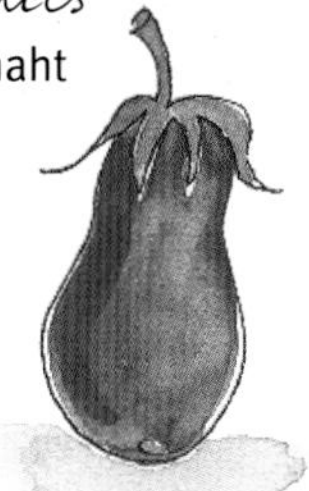

l'aubergine
loh•behr•jeen

le brocoli
luh bruh•kuh•lee

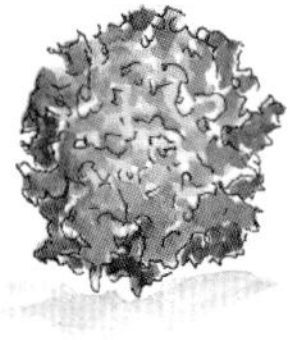

la frisée
lah free•zay

le céleri
luh sayl•ree

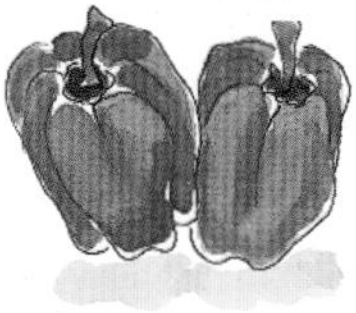

les poivrons
lay pwah•vrohn

le concombre
luh kohn•kohm•bruh

la trévise
lah tray•veez

Les Champignons

un cèpe
uhn sehp

les champignons
lay shahm•peen•yohn

les échalotes
layz ay•shah•luht

les girolles
lay jee•ruhl

l'ail
lah•yuh

le basilic
luh bah•zee•leek

une morille
oon moh•ree•yuh

les pleurotes
lay pluh•ruht

le thym
luh tehn

les truffes
lay troof

les mousserons
lay moos•rohn

les oignons
layz uhn•yohn

la ciboulette
lah see•boo•leht

Les Herbes

le romarin
luh ruh•mah•rehn

l'aneth
lah•neht

l'origan
loh•ree•gahn

la lavande
lah lah•vahn•duh

les herbes de Provence
layz ehrb duh proh•vahns

le laurier
luh luhr•ee•yay

le persil
luh pehr•see

la menthe
lah mahn•tuh

l'estragon
leh•strah•gohn

la sauge
lah soh•juh

51

Les Epices

le paprika
luh pah•pree•kah

la muscade
lah moos•kahd

la vanille
lah vah•nee•yuh

les poivrons
lay pwah•vrohn

la cannelle
lah kah•nehl

Les Condiments

le sel
luh sehl

le poivre
luh pwah•vruh

la moutarde
lah moo•tahrd

Tabasco
tah•bahs•koh

les câpres
lay kah•pruh

le ketchup
luh keht•chuhp

Les Céréales

le riz
luh ree

le riz sauvage
luh ree soh•vahj

le couscous
luh koos•koos

le blé
luh blay

l'avoine
lah•vwahn

Les Huiles

l'huile...
lweel

...d'olives
duh•leev

...d'arachide
dah•rah•sheed

...de noisettes
duh nwah•zeht

...de tournesol
duh toor•nuh•suhl

Les Préparations

bonne femme
buhn fahm

en croûte
ahn kroot

julienne
joo•lee•yeh•nuh

Alsacienne
ahl•sahs•yeh•nuh

Lyonnaise
lee•yuh•nehz

en brochette
ahn broh•sheht

Knowing how it's **prepared** will increase your comfort in ordering:
Alsacienne: with cabbage
Florentine: with spinach

les truffes
lay troof

Périgourdine
pay•ree•goor•deen

caramélisée
kara•may•lee•zay

forestière
foh•rehst•yehr

piquant
pee•kahn

Vichy
vee•shee

gratinée
grah•tee•nay

Florentine
floh•rahn•teen

Les Cuissons

Provençale
proh•vahn•sahl

véronique
vay•ruh•neek

sucré
soo•kray

au poivre
oh pwah•vruh

salé
sah•lay

How many ways can you **cook** a potato?

les pommes de terre . . .
à la vapeur: steamed
allumettes: shoestring
au four: baked
au gratin: with grated cheese
dauphines: with cream and cheese
frites: fried
gratinée: with cheese
Lyonnaise: with onions
parmentier: mashed with minced meat
purée: mashed
sautées: sautéed

Knowing how it's **cooked,** *les cuissons,* will increase your enjoyment (for meat see p. 79):

à l'étouffée: stewed
à la vapeur: steamed
beignet: fried
braisé: braised
chaud: hot
cru: raw
cuit au four: baked
daube: stewed
doré: toasted
en papillotte: steamed in a package
en roulade: rolled
farci: stuffed
fricassée: small morsels
frit: fried
froid: cold
fumé: smoked
grillé: grilled
mariné: marinated
piquant: hot, spicy
poché: poached
poêlé: pan-fried
rôti: roasted
sauté: sautéed

Les Sauces

Sauces are the backbone of French cooking. Menu choices often include the name of the sauce (*une **blanquette** de veau, une sole **meunière***). Included here are the **basic ingredients** that make up the sauces.

béchamel
bay•shah•mehl

beurre blanc
buhr blahn

blanquette
blahn•keht

Bordelaise
buhr•duh•lehz

Bourguignonne
boor•gheen•yuhn

Caen
kahn

Chantilly
shahn•tee•yee

chasseur
shah•suhr

aïoli
ah•ee•oh•lee

à la crème
ah•lah•kreh•muh

américaine
ameri•kehn

Béarnaise
bay•ahr•nehz

Bercy
behr•see

56

diable
dee•yah•bluh

financière
fee•nahn•see•yehr

hollandaise
uh•lahn•dehz

maître d' hôtel
meh•truh doh•tehl

mayonnaise
meh•yuh•nehz

meunière
muhn•yehr

mornay
mohr•nay

poivrade
pwah•vrahd

porto
pohr•toh

rémoulade
ray•moo•lahd

crème anglaise
krehm ahn•glehz

sauce au chocolat
sohs oh shuh•kuh•lah

vinaigrette
vee•neh•greht

57

BISTROT RESTAURANT

CHEZ PASTIS

SPÉCIALITÉS
RÉGIONALES

TÉLÉPHONE
FERMÉ
LE
DIMANCHE

CASSE-
CROÛTE

LE BEAUJOLAIS
NOUVEAU
EST
ARRIVÉ

. . . taking
time
to watch
the world
go by

"Morning pages"

Le Petit Déjeuner

luh puh•tee day•juh•nay

Les Viennoiseries

un croissant
uhn krwah•sahn

un bretzel aux raisins
uhn breht•sehl oh reh•zehn

une brioche
oon bree•yush

un pain aux raisins
uhn pehn oh reh•zehn

un chausson aux pommes
uhn shoh•sohn oh puh•muh

un pain au chocolat
unh pehn oh shuh•kuh•lah

les viennoiseries: small breakfast breads, originally a tradition of Vienna

un palmier
uhn pahl•mee•yay

le grille-pain
luh gree•yuh pehn

les toasts
lay toast

un pain brioché
uhn pehn bree•yuh•shay

Le Petit Déjeuner

les fruits
lay frwee

une tartine
oon tahr•teen

du beurre
doo buhr

de la confiture
duh lah kohn•fee•toor

un jus d'orange
uhn joo duh•rahnj

la marmelade
lah mahr•muh•lahd

un yaourt
uhn yah•oort

müesli
moos•lee

un oeuf à la coque
uhn uhf ah lah kuhk

du lait
doo lay

61

Les Cafés

un express
uhn ehks•prehs

un déca
uhn day•kah

un café au lait
uhn kah•fay oh lay

un double express
uhn doobl ehks•prehs

Beverages, *les boissons*, served at the bar are as much as **half the price** of those served in the dining room or on the terrace.

un café américain
uhn kah•fay ameri•kehn

un petit crème
uhn puh•tee krehm

un cappuccino
uhn kah•poo•chee•noh

un grand crème
uhn grahn krehm

Boissons Chaudes   Le Thé

un chocolat chaud
uhn shuh•kuh•lah shoh

un citron chaud
uhn see•trohn shoh

le sucre
luh soo•kruh

la saccharine
lah sah•kah•reen

un thé . . . nature
uhn tay nah•toor

. . . citron
see•trohn

. . . au lait
oh lay

le miel
luh mee•yehl

une tisane
oon tee•zahn

Favorite cafés

un "Resto"
shorthand for restaurant

café sitting is a
full-time job

Le Déjeuner

luh day•juh•nay

Les Oeufs

une omelette nature
oon uhm•leht nah•toor

les oeufs au plat
layz uhf oh plah

- aux fines herbes
  oh feenz ehr•buh

- aux champignons
  oh shahm•peen•yohn

Eggs are most often eaten for lunch or a light dinner with a green salad and cheese.

- au fromage
  oh fruh•mahj

- au jambon
  oh jahm•bohn

les oeufs brouillés
layz uhf broo•yay

un oeuf dur
uhn uhf door

un soufflé
uhn soo•flay

Les Salades

la vinaigrette
lah vee•neh•greht

les carottes râpées
lay kah•ruht rah•pay

une niçoise
oon nee•swahz

la vinaigrette or la sauce: oil, vinegar, mustard. It's delicious. Don't ask for other choices—there aren't any!

les tomates et mozzarella
lay toh•maht ay moht•zah•rel•la

une salade verte
oon sah•lahd vehrt

le pain: bread is served automatically. Note: there is no bread plate. Put it directly on the table; it's OK!

un chèvre chaud
uhn sheh•vruh shoh

67

Les Crêpes

une pizza
oon peet•zah

une gaufre
oon goh•fruh

les crêpes:
pancakes made
with white flour

les galettes:
pancakes made
with buckwheat

une crêpe salée:
(salted)
as a main course

une crêpe sucrée:
(sugared)
as a dessert

une crêpe salée
oon krehp sah•lay

une quiche
oon keesh

une tourte
oon toort

une crêpe sucrée
oon krehp soo•kray

Les Sandwiches

un croque-monsieur
uhn kruhk muhs•yuh

=

le fromage
luh fruh•mahj

+

le jambon
luh jahm•bohn

un croque-madame
uhn kruhk mah•dahm

Beware: cold sandwiches are always made with butter or mayonnaise.

un panini
uhn pah•nini

un pâté
uhn pah•tay

un sandwich mixte
uhn sahn•dweech meekst

un steak haché
uhn stayk ah•shay

les chips
lay sheeps

les cornichons
lay kuhr•nee•shohn

69

Les Boissons Fraîches

un citron pressé
uhn see•trohn preh•say

un jus de tomate
uhn joo duh toh•maht

un café glacé
uhn kah•fay glah•say

un orangina
uhn uh•rahn•jee•nah

les glaçons
lay glah•sohn

un thé glacé
uhn tay glah•say

un Perrier
uhn pehr•yay

l'eau plate
loh plaht

. . . gazeuse
gah•zuhz

une bière
oon bee•yehr

une pression
oon prehs•yohn

les boissons fraîches:
cold drinks

l'eau plate:
flat water, no bubbles

l'eau gazeuse:
with bubbles

Bottles of water:
une bouteille (liter)
une demi (1/2 liter)
un quart (1/4 liter)

les bières françaises:
Kronenbourg
Pilsen
Stella d'Artois

une bouteille
oon boo•teh•yuh

un coca

un Schweppes
uhn shweps

Don't be shy to ask for a carafe.

un coca (lite)
uhn koh•kah
(lite)

une carafe d'eau
oon kah•rahf doh

un pichet (de vin)
uhn pee•shay (duh vehn)

71

Memorable meals...

A complete French meal includes several courses.

les apéritifs: before dinner drinks
les entrées: starters
les pains: bread
les soupes: soup
les plats: main courses
  les volailles: poultry
  les viandes: meat
  les gibiers: wild game
  les fruits de mer: seafood
  les poissons: fish
les fromages: cheese
les desserts: dessert
les pâtisseries: pastry
les vins: wine

enjoy the differences ...
try something new every day

Le Dîner

luh dee•nay

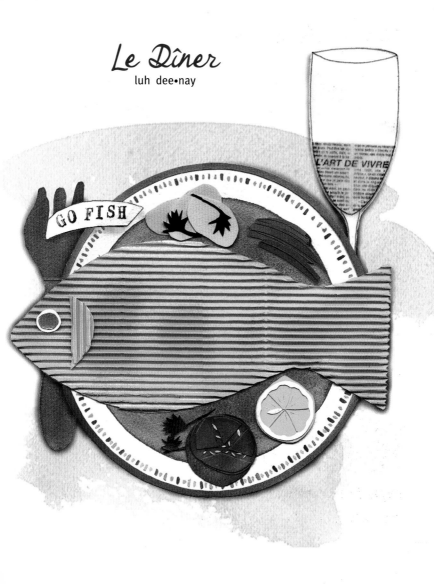

Les Apéritifs

vin blanc

CRÈME de Cassis BEAUNE

un kir
uhn keer

champagne

CRÈME de Cassis BEAUNE

un kir royal
uhn keer roy•ahl

du champagne
doo shahm•pahn•yuh

When invited to a home for dinner (never before 8 p.m.), the cocktail hour is very short, as are the drinks and snacks. Dinner and wine are the main event.

un porto
uhn pohr•toh

les canapés
lay kah•nah•pay

les crackers
lay krah•kehr

les olives
layz uh•leev

74

Les Entrées

les grenouilles
lay gruh•noo•yuh

les asperges
layz ahs•pehrj

les escargots
layz ehs•kahr•goh

une salade verte
oon sah•lahd vehrt

Les entrées, first course starters, are often the specialties of the season or region.

You can always ask for a green salad, *une salade verte,* if you want to start simply.

Often I order two starters to save room for dessert.

...de canard
duh kah•nahr

un foie gras...
uhn fwah grah

...d'oie
dwah

un melon au porto
uhn muh•lohn oh pohr•toh

Les Pains

une baguette
oon bah•gheht

une ficelle
oon fee•sehl

une boule
oon boo•luh

un épi
uhn ay•pee

un pain aux noix
uhn pehn oh nwah

un pain aux olives
uhn pehn ohz uh•leev

une tresse
oon trehs

une couronne
oon koo•ruhn

les petits pains
lay puh•tee pehn

une fougasse
oon foo•gahs

un pain de campagne
uhn pehn duh kahm•pahn•yuh

Les Soupes

**une soupe,
un potage:** soup

un velouté: a creamy soup

un bouillon: water in which chicken or vegetables have been cooked

une julienne: vegetables in water

une bisque: soup made with shellfish or seafood

une soupe de poisson: soup made with fish

une gratinée Lyonnaise
oon grah•tee•nay lee•yuh•nehz

une vichyssoise
oon vee•shee•swahz

un pistou
uhn pees•too

Les Volailles

un poulet
uhn poo•lay

une poularde: pullet
un poulet: chicken
un poussin: spring chicken
un chapon: capon
un coq: rooster

Beware!
The French love to eat all the parts. You may want to pay special attention to these:

les andouillettes:
tripes* sausage
du boudin:
blood sausage
la cervelle:
brains
le foie:
liver
la langue:
tongue
le ris de veau:
sweetbreads
les rognons:
kidneys
***les tripes:**
intestines

l'oie
lwah

une pintade
oon pehn•tahd

For sauces, preparations, and cooking styles, see p. 54–57.

une dinde
oon dehn•duh

un coq au vin
uhn kuhk oh vehn

un canard farci aux pommes
uhn kah•nar far•see oh puhm

Les Viandes

le boeuf
luh buhf

le veau
luh voh

What cut would you prefer?

un carré: rack
un chateaubriand: porter-house steak
un civet: wine stew
les côtes: chops
une entrecôte: sirloin
l'épaule: shoulder
une escalope de: cutlet of
un filet: boneless cut
un gigot: leg
un haché: ground
le jambon: ham
les médaillons: tenderloins
un paillard de: a fine cut of
un rôti: roast
les saucisses: sausage
un steak tartare: raw chopped steak
suprême de: breast of

le porc
luh pohr

un cassoulet
uhn kah•soo•lay

l'agneau
lahn•yoh

How do you want it cooked?

bien cuit: well done
à point: medium
rosé: medium rare
saignant: rare
bleu: barely warm

le lapin
luh lah•pehn

un civet de lapin
uhn see•veh duh lah•pehn

79

Les Gibiers

une bécasse
oon bay•kahs

une caille
oon kah•yuh

un perdreau
uhn pehr•droh

un lapin
uhn lah•pehn

un chevreuil
uhn shuh•vruh•yuh

une grive
oon greev

un lièvre
uhn lee•yeh•vruh

un faisan
uhn feh•zahn

un sanglier
uhn sahn•glee•yay

un civet* de lièvre
uhn see•vay duh
lee•yeh•vruh

les gibiers: wild
game, available in
season, usually in
the fall.

*un civet: wine stew

Les Fruits De Mer

un crabe
uhn krahb

les huîtres
layz wee•truh

les crevettes roses
lay kruh•veht rohz

les coquilles Saint-Jacques
lay kuh•kee•yuh sehn jahk

les crevettes grises
lay kruh•veht greez

une langoustine
oon lahn•goos•teen

les palourdes
lay pah•loord

un homard
uhn oh•mahr

les moules
lay moo•luh

81

Les Poissons

Knowing the **characteristics** of your fish choices, *les poissons,* will create fewer surprises. Example: #1=white fish, #4=oily, #19=served in slices

l'aile de raie: 1, 4, 7, 11, 19

les anchois: 2, 4, 11, 14

le bar/loup: 1, 6, 10, 12, 14, or 15

le cabillaud: 1, 6, 8, 10, 14

le colin: 1, 6, 8. 10, 12, 14, or 15

la daurade: 1, 6, 8, 10, 14, or 15

le flétan: 1, 6, 8, 10, 12, 14

le hareng: 2, 4, 9, 11, 13, 17

la lotte: 1, 5, 8, 10, 13, 14

le maquereau: 2, 4, 7, 13, 17

le merlan: 1, 6, 10, 13, 15

la morue: 1, 5, 8, 11, 13, 18

la perche: 1, 6, 10, 12, 15

la rascasse: 20

les rougets: 3, 6, 7, 11, 13, 15

le Saint-Pierre: 1, 5, 7, 10, 12, 14, or 15

le sandre: 1, 6, 7, 10, 12, 14

les sardines: 2, 4, 9, 11, 13, 17

le saumon: 3, 5, 7, 11, 13, 16, or 19

la sole: 1, 6, 8, 10, 12, 15

le thon: 3, 4, 8, 11, 13, 16, or 19

la truite: 2, 6, 7, 10, 15

le turbot: 1, 4, 8, 11, 13, 18

Characteristics

1. white
2. grey
3. pink
4. oily, very fatty
5. fatty
6. non-fat
7. bony
8. no bones
9. edible bones

Flavor & Texture

10. subtle
11. strong
12. flaky
13. dense

Usual Servings

14. filet
15. whole
16. steak
17. several small fish
18. pieces or chunks
19. slices
20. soup

un saumon
uhn soh•mohn

une daurade
oon duh•rahd

une sole
oon suhl

For sauces,
preparations, and
cooking styles,
see p. 54–57.

une bouillabaisse
oon boo•yah•behs

l'aile de raie
lehl duh reh

les anchois
layz ahn•shwah

un rouget
uhn roo•jay

un turbot
uhn toor•boh

un sandre à l'oseille
uhn sahn•druh
ah loh•zeh•yuh

une fricassée de langoustines
oon free•kah•say duh lahn•goos•teen

Les Fromages

la chèvre
lah sheh•vruh

Here is a sampling of 15 french cheeses, but don't forget there are 385 other choices. Cheeses are made from goat, sheep, or cow's milk.

la brebis
lah bruh•bee

un Sainte-Maure
uhn sehnt mohr

fleur de maquis
fluhr duh mah•kee

les crottins de chavignol
lay kruh•tehn duh shah•veen•yuhl

un roquefort
uhn ruhk•fohr

un valençay
uhn vah•lahn•say

fromage Corse
fruh•mahj kuhr•suh

la crème fraîche
lah krehm freh•shuh

le plateau
luh plah•toh

84

un camembert
uhn kah•mahm•behr

la vache
lah vah•shuh

le brie
luh bree

du gruyère
doo groo•yehr

l'emmental
leh•mahn•tahl

du cantal
doo kahn•tahl

le pont l'évêque
luh pohn lay•veh•kuh

du beaufort
doo boh•fohr

un reblochon
uhn ruh•bluh•shohn

le neufchâtel
luh nuh•shah•tehl

un bleu d'Auvergne
uhn bluh doh•vehrn•yuh

un livarot
uhn lee•vah•roh

85

Les Desserts

les profiteroles
lay pruh•fee•tuh•ruhl

une tarte . . .
oon tahrt

. . . *aux poires*
oh pwahr

. . . *aux pommes*
oh puh•muh

une crème caramel
oon krehm kah•rah•mehl

To order a piece
or slice of tart
or cake, ask for
une part de . . .

une glace
oon glahs

. . . *aux fraises*
oh frehz

un clafoutis
uhn klah•foo•tee

86

...à la banane
ah lah bah•nah•nuh

les crêpes suzette
lay krehp soo•zeht

une île flottante
oon eel fluh•tahn•tuh

une salade de fruits
oon sah•lahd duh frwee

...aux abricots
ohz ah•bree•koh

une crème brûlée
oon krehm broo•lay

un vacherin
uhn vahsh•rehn

Les Pâtisseries

un sablé aux fruits
uhn sah•blay oh frwee

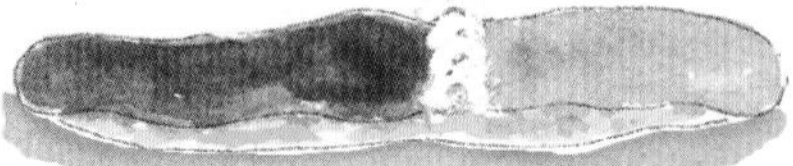

un éclair
uhn ay•klehr

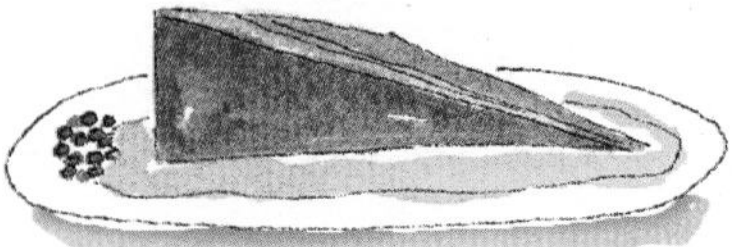

un gâteau au chocolat
uhn gah•toh oh shuh•kuh•lah

une nougatine
oon noo•gah•teen

un savarin
uhn sah•vah•rehn

un mado
uhn mah•doh

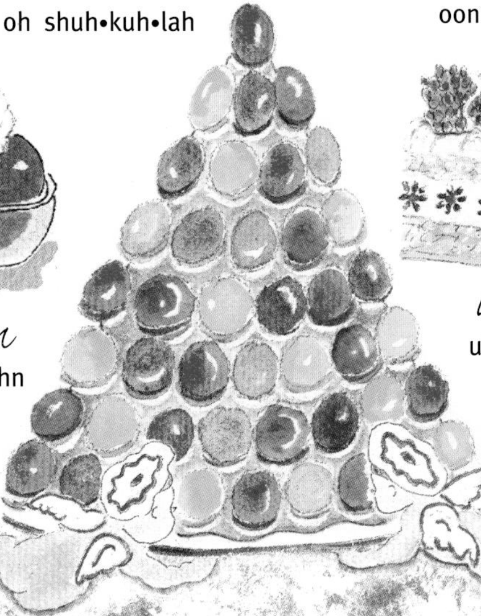

les macarons de Chez Ladurée
lay mah•kah•rohn duh shay lah•doo•ray

une religieuse
oon ruh•leej•yuhz

un soufflé
uhn soo•flay

une mousse
oon moos

une tarte . . .

. . . à l'orange
ah luh•rahnj

un Saint-Honoré
uhn sehnt uh•nuh•ray

un Paris-Brest
uhn pah•ree brehst

. . . aux fruits
oh frwee

un mille-feuille
uhn meel fuh•yuh

In a fine
restaurant,
small cookies
and sweets
are served
with coffee.

un verre
uhn vehr

un pichet
uhn pee•shay

rouge
rooj

blanc
blahn

rosé
roh•zay

La Carte des Vins

un verre: a glass, 12.5 cl* = 4 oz.
un pichet: a pitcher, 50 cl = 17 oz.
une bouteille: a bottle, 75 cl =
6 glasses = 25 oz.
une demi: ½ bottle
un vin de table: house wine
*centiliter

lah kahrt day vehn

une bouteille *une demi*
oon boo•teh•yuh oon duh•mee

Les Vins

Bourgogne
boor•guhn•yuh

le tire-bouchon
luh teer boo•shohn

le bouchon
luh boo•shohn

Champagne
shahm•pahn•yuh

Beaujolais
boh•juh•lay

Chardonnay
shahr•duh•nay

Bordeaux
bohr•doh

One for you, two for me

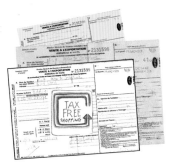

Détaxe: a refund of 13%–16% of the 26% tax included in all purchases

You must spend about 200 *euros* in any one store at any one time.

This refund can be declared when you leave the country.

Before airport check in, go to the *détaxe* desk and be prepared to show your purchases in order to qualify for the refund.

Once this form has been validated, you can either mail the pink copy directly to the merchant, who will credit your credit card, or find the **Cash Back** desk for an immediate cash refund.

DIANE VERNAY
14, rue Faubourg
St Honoré

Shopping

Le Shopping

Le Shopping

Les soldes, sales, are traditionally from mid-January to February and mid-July to August.

en solde: on sale

rabais: a percentage off the regular price

une remise: reduction in price for selected customers

promotion: introductory price for a new product

une griffe: a label or designer name

dégriffé: designer items without the label for less money

fins de séries: end-of-season sale

réciproque: resale shop of nearly new clothes

vêtements occasion: second-hand clothes

vente en gros: wholesale

vente au détail: retail

vente aux professionnels: sales to the trade

vente aux particuliers: sales also to individuals at retail

en solde
ahn suhl•duh

Look for this book, available only in France

Paris Pas Cher
pah•ree pah shehr

pas cher: not expensive

cher: expensive

trop cher: too expensive

dégriffé
day•gree•fay

Dans La Vitrine

1. *Sonner*

2. *Entrée Libre*

3.

"Bonjour, Madame"
bohn•joor mah•dahm

4.

"Au Revoir, Madame"
oh ruh•vwahr mah•dahm

5. *La Carte Bleue*
lah kahr•tuh bluh

6. *détaxe*
day•tahks

---

la vitrine: shop window

1. *sonner:* don't be afraid to ring the bell

2. *entrée libre:* browsers welcome

3. *la politesse:* manners No matter what kind of shop you enter, it's proper to say *"Bonjour, Madame (Monsieur)."*

4. In parting it's proper to say *"Au revoir, merci Madame (Monsieur),"* especially if you've been browsing and not buying. Notice how the French kind of singsong the greetings. Try it, it's fun.

5. *La Carte Bleue:* VISA card (accepted everywhere)

les cartes de crédit: credit cards

6. *détaxe:* tax-free

7. *espèces:* cash

Les Boutiques

Chez: used for naming shops and restaurants, "the house of . . ."

CHEZ COCO

FERMÉ

une boutique
oon boo•teek

OUVERT • FERMÉ

10h   a   7h le soir

FERMÉ à déjeuner

13h   à   14h

la vendeuse
lah vahn•duhz

AU PR

MAGASIN de

Les Magasins

LE WEEK-END
MAGASIN de SPORT • RELAX • VOYAGE

un magasin
uhn mah•gah•zehn

un grand magasin
uhn grahn mah•gah•zehn

HEURES d'OUVERTURE

9h 30 à 6h 30 le soir

SANS INTERRUPTION
open all day

Once you've made your choices, paying is the most complicated part.

1. Find a sales clerk who writes up the sale.
2. Leave your purchases with the clerk.
3. Find *LA CAISSE* and pay.
4. Return with your paid sales slip.
5. Recover your purchases . . .

Don't forget: You can accumulate all your sales slips for the day and ask for your *détaxe* (see p. 92).

Note: All shops are closed for *les jours feriés,* holidays, on May 1, July 14, December 25, and January 1.

tirez
tee•ray

ouvert
oo•vehr

poussez
poo•say

fermé
fehr•may

l'escalator
lehs•kah•lah•tohr

l'ascenseur
lah•sahn•suhr

CENTRE COMMERCIAL

E. LECLERC   HYPERMARCHÉ

sahn•truh
kuh•mehrs•yal

les CADDIES

HEURES d'OUVERTURE

Sans interruption
Lundi - Samedi

CONTINENT MONDEVILLE

SPORT   194,00
FRUIT   28,00
PAPETERIE   +4,50
          TOT 298,55

Carte bancaire 298,55
A RENDRE   ,00

NOMBRE d'ARTICLES 2

1 EURO = 6,55 FF
TOTAL en EURO   42,111
+ MERCI de VOTRE VISITE +

le reçu
luh ruh•soo

LA CAISSE

lah keh•suh

Les caddies, shopping
carts, require a *1 euro*
deposit, redeemable
upon return.

Be prepared to pack
your own groceries.
Most of the time the
French just throw it all
back in the cart.

un hypermarché
uhn ee•pehr•mahr•shay

Les Marchés

le marché aux timbres
luh mahr•shay oh tehm•bruh

le marché Saint-Pierre, Paris
luh mahr•shay sehn pee•yehr pah•ree

le marché aux fleurs
luh mahr•shay oh fluhr

un antiquaire
uhn ahn•tee•kehr

Dépôt Vente   day•poh vahnt
A warehouse selling "stuff" left on consignment; low-end antiques, *brocante*. Sometimes treasures can be found.

le marché aux puces
luh mahr•shay oh poos

les passages - les galeries
lay pah•sahj   lay gahl•ree

un bouquiniste
uhn boo•kee•neest

CADEAUX

Gifts to buy and

...where
to buy
them

toys, *un magasin de jouets*
uhn mah•gah•zehn duh joo•way

clothing, *un magasin de vêtements*
uhn mah•gah•zehn duh veht•mahn

lingerie, *un magasin de lingerie*
uhn mah•gah•zehn duh lehn•juh•ree

shoes, *un magasin de chaussures*
uhn mah•gah•zehn duh shoh•soor

leather goods, *une maroquinerie*
oon mah•ruh•keen•ree

jewelry, *une bijouterie*
oon bee•joo•tree

music, *un magasin de disques*
uhn mah•gah•zehn duh deesk

sporting goods, *un magasin de sport*
uhn mah•gah•zehn duh spohr

artwork, *une galerie d'art*
oon gahl•ree dahr

Pour Les Enfants

une poupée
oon poo•pay

un garçon
uhn gahr•sohn

une fille
oon fee•yuh

un livre
uhn lee•vruh

les tailles:
sizes

nouveau-né:
newborn

0–24 mois:
ask by months

2 ans–14 ans:
ask by age

un camion
uhn kah•mee•yohn

un puzzle
uhn puh•zehl

une toupie
oon too•pee

vêtements d'enfants
veht•mahn dahn•fahn

103

Les Vêtements Pour Femmes

un ensemble
uhn ahn•sahm•bluh

une veste
oon vehst

une jupe
oon joop

Women's sizes:	
France	U.S.
34/36	2/4 petite
38/40	6/8 small
42/44	10/12 med.
46/48	14/16 large

un bustier
uhn boos•tee•yay

une chemise de nuit
oon shuh•meez duh nwee

un soutien-gorge
uhn soot•yehn guhr•juh

une blouse
oon blooz

les mules
lay mool

un slip
uhn sleep

un cardigan
uhn kahr•dee•gahn

104

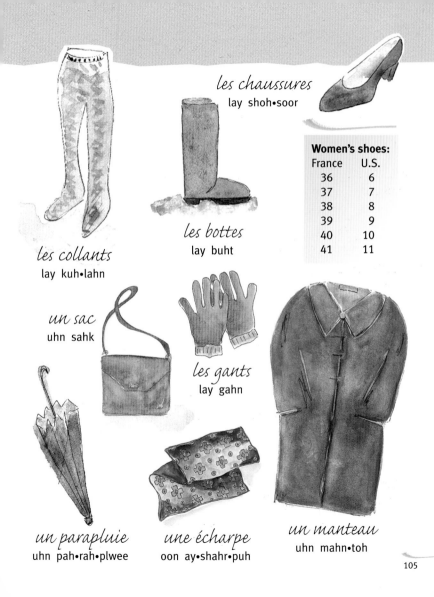

les chaussures
lay shoh•soor

Women's shoes:
France	U.S.
36	6
37	7
38	8
39	9
40	10
41	11

les bottes
lay buht

les collants
lay kuh•lahn

un sac
uhn sahk

les gants
lay gahn

un parapluie
uhn pah•rah•plwee

une écharpe
oon ay•shahr•puh

un manteau
uhn mahn•toh

105

Les Vêtements Unisex

un t-shirt
uhn tee shuhrt

un short
uhn shohrt

un pull-over
uhn pool•oh•vehr

Men's Shirts

France	U.S.
36	14
37	14 1/2
38	15
39	15 1/2
40	16
41	16 1/2

les chaussettes
lay shoh•seht

un gilet
uhn jee•lay

Men's Shoes

France	U.S.
39 1/2	7
40	7 1/2
41	8
42	9
43	10
44 1/2	11

une écharpe
oon ay•shahr•puh

un chapeau
uhn shah•poh

Les Vêtements Pour Hommes

une veste
oon vehs•tuh

une chemise
oon shuh•meez

un costume
uhn kuhs•toom

un pantalon
uhn pahn•tah•lohn

un blouson
uhn bloo•zohn

Men's clothes	
France	U.S.
46	36
48	38
50	40
52	42
54	44
56	46

une cravate
oon krah•vaht

une ceinture
oon sehn•toor

un noeud papillon
uhn nuh pah•pee•yohn

un jean
uhn jeen

Les Couleurs

rouge
rooj

bordeaux
bohr•doh

rose
rohz

orange
uh•rahnj

jaune
joh•nuh

vert
vehr

bleu
bluh

turquoise
toor•kwahz

pourpre
poor•pruh

lavande
lah•vahn•duh

brun
bruhn

beige
behj

noir
nwahr

gris
gree

blanc
blahn

argenté
ahr•jahn•tay

doré
doh•ray

clair . . . foncé
klehr . . . fohn•say

Pour Les Artistes

les pinceaux
lay pehn•soh

fournitures pour artistes
foor•nee•toor poor ahr•teest

un stylo
uhn stee•loh

les aquarelles
layz ah•kwah•rehl

les pastels
lay pahs•tehl

la peinture
lah pehn•toor

un cahier à dessin
uhn kah•yay ah deh•sehn

Pour Les Sportifs

une raquette de tennis
oon rah•keht duh teh•nees

un vélo
uhn vay•loh

un skateboard
uhn skeht•buhrd

des balles
day bahl

un sac de golf
uhn sahk duh guhlf

les rollers
lay ruh•lehr

l'équipement de ski
lay•keep•mahn duh skee

110

L'Alimentation

une épicerie:
oon ay•pees•ree
a small
grocery store

Food, *l'alimentation,* is found in these specialty shops or at the market, *au marché.*

bread, *une boulangerie*
    oon boo•lahnj•ree

candy, *une confiserie*
    oon kohn•feez•ree

cheese, *une crémerie*
    oon krehm•ree
    une fromagerie
    oon fruh•mahj•ree

chocolate, *un chocolatier*
    oon shuh•kuh•laht•yay

fish, *une poissonnerie*
    oon pwah•shun•ree

fruits and vegetables,
    une fruiterie
    frwee•tree

ice cream, *un glacier*
    uhn glahs•yay

meat, *une boucherie*
    oon boosh•ree
    une charcuterie
    oon shar•koo•tree

pastry, *une pâtisserie*
    oon pah•tees•ree

wine, *un caviste*
    uhn kah•veest

Au Marché

frwee•tree

un kilo
uhn kee•loh

une livre
oon lee•vruh

les halles
lay ahl

le marché:
outdoor market

les halles:
a covered market,
usually open one
day a week.

In the village or
local neighbor-
hood, small food
shops usually
close between
1–3 p.m.

une bouteille
oon boo•teh•yuh

le marché
luh mahr•shay

cent grammes
sahn grah•muh

112

une poignée de . . .
oon pwahn•yay duh

du beurre
doo buhr

un bocal de . . .
uhn boh•kahl duh

une tasse
oon tahs

Measurements:

un kilo:
2.2 lbs.
un demi (½) kilo:
1.1 lbs.
une livre:
½ kilo, 1.1 lbs
une poignée:
a handful
un litre:
1 quart or 4 cups
cent (100) grammes:
¼ lb.
une tasse: 1 cup or
¼ litre
un quart de beurre:
250 grams, ½ lb.

une boîte de . . .
oon bwaht duh

une part de . . .
oon pahr duh

une demi-douzaine
oon duh•mee doo•zeh•nuh

un morceau de . . .
uhn mohr•soh duh

une tranche de . . .
oon trahn•shuh duh

113

A La Maison

Celsius		Fahrenheit
120°	=	275°
150°	=	325°
180°	=	400°
200°	=	425°
230°	=	500°

le four
luh foor

un réfrigérateur
uhn ray•free•jay•rah•tuhr

le séchoir
luh say•shwahr

le lave-linge
luh lahv lehnj

le lave-vaisselle
luh lahv veh•sehl

le grille-pain
luh gree•yuh pehn

un aspirateur
uhn ahs•pee•rah•tuhr

un balai
uhn bah•leh

un gant
uhn gahn

un tablier
uhn tah•blee•yay

une pelle
oon pehl

un rideau de douche
uhn ree•doh duh doosh

Housewares:
une droguerie
(not to be confused with a
drugstore, **une pharmacie**)

Small electrical appliances:
**un magasin
d'électroménager**

Furniture:
un magasin de meubles

etrt de la Table

Fine tableware:
Art de la table
selling upscale tabletop
accessories

Or ask for **un magasin
de . . .**

. . . **cristal,** crystal
. . . **argenterie,** silver
. . . **porcelaine,** fine china
. . . **verrerie,** glassware

La Batterie De Cuisine

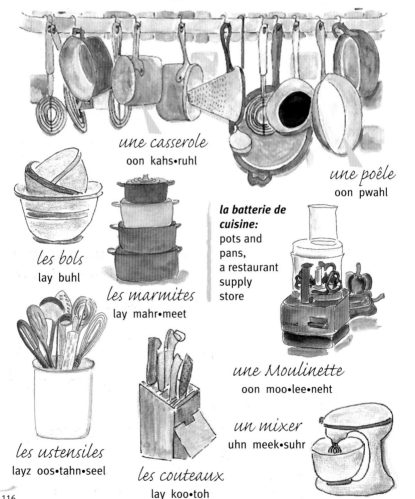

une casserole
oon kahs•ruhl

une poêle
oon pwahl

les bols
lay buhl

les marmites
lay mahr•meet

la batterie de cuisine: pots and pans, a restaurant supply store

une Moulinette
oon moo•lee•neht

un mixer
uhn meek•suhr

les ustensiles
layz oos•tahn•seel

les couteaux
lay koo•toh

116

Bricolage

QUINCAILLERIE
kehn•kah•yuh•ree

OUVERT 8 à 20
7
JOURS

bricolage:
do-it-yourself

quincaillerie:
hardware store

la peinture
lah pehn•toor

un rouleau à peinture
uhn roo•loh ah pehn•toor

une clé à molette
oon klay ah muh•leht

une scie
oon see

un clou
uhn kloo

un marteau
uhn mahr•toh

un tournevis
uhn toor•nuh•vees

une vis
oon vees

une pince
oon pehn•suh

117

Les Chiffres

0	*zéro*	zay•roh
1	*un, une*	uhn, oon
2	*deux*	duh
3	*trois*	trwah
4	*quatre*	kah•truh
5	*cinq*	sehnk
6	*six*	sees
7	*sept*	seht
8	*huit*	weet
9	*neuf*	nuhf
10	*dix*	dees
11	*onze*	ohnz
12	*douze*	dooz
13	*treize*	trehz
14	*quatorze*	kah•tuhrz
15	*quinze*	kehnz
16	*seize*	sehz
17	*dix-sept*	dees seht
18	*dix-huit*	dees weet
19	*dix-neuf*	dees nuhf
20	*vingt*	vehn
30	*trente*	trahnt
40	*quarante*	kah•rahnt
50	*cinquante*	sehn•kahnt
60	*soixante*	swah•sahnt
70	*soixante-dix* (60 + 10)	swah•sahnt dees
80	*quatre-vingts* (4 x 20)	kah•truh vehn
90	*quatre-vingt-dix* (4 x 20 + 10)	kah•truh vehn dees
100	*cent*	sahn
500	*cinq cents*	sehn sahn
1000	*mille*	meel

L'Argent

un DISTRIBUTEUR

uhn dees•tree•boo•tuhr

Les distributeurs: Cash machines are the easiest way to get cash using your ATM card and PIN code. *Distributeurs* are found at every bank and most post offices.

Le Bureau de Change is your next best bet. Note: the rate you receive is the one listed under *vente*.

There's no such thing as **"no commission"**; it's included in the rate.

Les Cartes Bleues: VISA cards are accepted in the *métro*, on the *autoroute*, in taxis displaying the cards, and at virtually every restaurant and hotel.

"Change" Euros

les billets
lay bee•yay

les pièces
lay pee•yehs

Although the French franc has become a collector's item, you can still redeem them at the **Banque de France**.

les euros
layz uhr•oh

1 et 2 euros

10, 20, et 50 cents

1, 2, et 5 cents

La Communication

une télécarte
oon tay•lay•kahrt

un portable
uhn por•tah•bluh

Une télécarte:
a telephone card
is imperative
for almost all
phone booths.
**Une carte
téléphonique** with
a PIN code is
good at hotels and
phone booths.
Buy one in a
tabac, at **la poste,**
or at a kiosk
(p. 126).

une cabine
oon kah•been

l'homme d'affaires
luhm dah•fehr

La Communication:

To call the USA from France:
001 + area code + number

**For other international calls
from France:**
00 + country code + number

To call France from the USA:
011 (international)
+33 (country code)
+1 (region code, see map)
+42 45 46 47 (eight digits)

For e-mail: for local access, use
a worldwide server like AOL,
Compuserve, or Hotmail

For portable phones: you must
have a worldwide service or
rent a cell phone

un cybercafé
uhn see•behr kah•fay

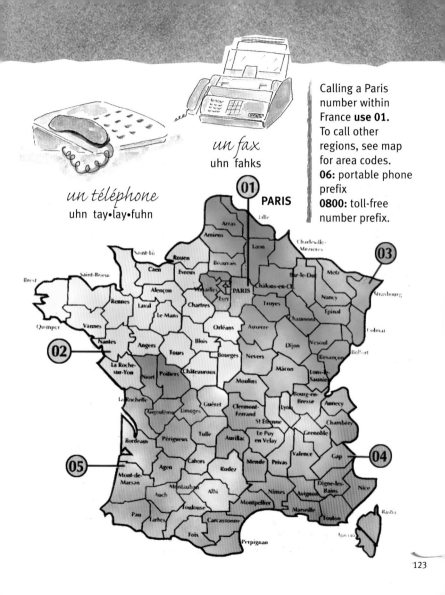

un fax
uhn fahks

un téléphone
uhn tay•lay•fuhn

Calling a Paris number within France **use 01.** To call other regions, see map for area codes.
06: portable phone prefix
0800: toll-free number prefix.

01
PARIS

03

02

05

04

Arras
Lille
Amiens
Saint-Lô
Rouen
Beauvais
Laon
Charleville-Mézières
Caen
Evreux
Metz
Brest
Saint-Brieuc
Alençon
Versailles
PARIS
Châlons-en-Ch.
Nancy
Strasbourg
Rennes
Laval
Chartres
Evry
Troyes
Epinal
Le Mans
Orléans
Auxerre
Chaumont
Colmar
Quimper
Vannes
Nantes
Angers
Blois
Dijon
Vesoul
Belfort
Tours
Bourges
Nevers
Besançon
La Roche-sur-Yon
Châteauroux
Mâcon
Lons-le-Saunier
Niort
Poitiers
Moulins
Bourg-en-Bresse
La Rochelle
Guéret
Clermont-Ferrand
Lyon
Annecy
Angoulême
Limoges
St Etienne
Chambéry
Bordeaux
Périgueux
Tulle
Aurillac
Le Puy en Velay
Grenoble
Agen
Cahors
Rodez
Mende
Privas
Valence
Gap
Mont-de-Marsan
Montauban
Albi
Nîmes
Avignon
Digne-les-Bains
Nice
Auch
Montpellier
Marseille
Bastia
Pau
Tarbes
Toulouse
Carcassonne
Toulon
Fox
Perpignan
Ajaccio

123

La Poste

le bureau de poste
luh boo•roh duh puhst

un colis
uhn kuh•lee

Un colis, a package, can be sent by . . .

Mail boxes are discreetly located on building exteriors.

une boîte aux lettres
oon bwaht oh leh•truh

une carte postale
oon kahrt puhs•tahl

124

Le Courrier

l'enveloppe
lahn•vluhp

les timbres
lay tehm•bruh

le cachet
luh kah•shay

l'adresse
lah•drehs

PRIORITAIRE
PRIORITY

M. et Mme Robert Larue
12, rue (street) de la Pompe
75016 (zip code) Paris, France

une lettre
oon leh•truh

un coursier
uhn koor•see•yay

robertlarue@hotmail

un e-mail
uhn ee•mehl

un ordinateur
uhn uhr•dee•nah•tuhr

Postcards to send

le bureau de poste
luh boo•roh duh puhst
post office

les timbres
lay tehm•bruh
stamps

les cartes postales
lay kahrt puhs•tahl
postcards

pour les Etats-Unis
poor layz ay•tah•zoo•nee
for the United States

un kiosque
uhn kee•yuhsk

126

Le Tabac

un verre de vin
uhn vehr duh vehn

un café
uhn kah•fay

un tabac
uhn tah•bah

des cigarettes
day see•gah•reht

les magazines
lay mah•gah•zeen

Bar-Tabac: telephone cards, cigarettes, newspapers, stamps, *métro* tickets, and drinks are sold here, as well as simple meals and coffee.

un film
uhn feelm

un journal
uhn joor•nahl

un timbre
uhn tehm•bruh

un sandwich
uhn sahnd•weech

Les Services Photo

les tirages
lay tee•rahj

une pellicule
oon peh•lee•kool

les diapos
lay dee•ah•poh

une pile
oon peel

appareil-photo numérique: a digital camera. Supplies found at large photo stores.

une disquette
oon dees•keht

une photocopieuse
oon foh•toh•kuhp•yuhz

A4
A3

A4 = 8.5" x 11"

A3 = 11" x 17"

les photos d'identité
lay foh•toh dee•dahn•tee•tay

128

un crayon
uhn kreh•yohn

une règle
oon reh•gluh

du papier à lettres
doo pahp•yay ah leh•truh

une papeterie:
paper shop
une fournitures de bureau:
office supply store
une librairie:
book store
une bibliothèque:
library

3 centimètres: 1 inch
1 mètre: 1 yard or 3 ft.

un livre
uhn lee•vruh

les trombones
lay trohm•buhn

une agrafeuse
oon ah•grah•fuhz

des ciseaux
day see•zoh

le scotch
luh skuhtch

une librairie
oon lee•breh•ree

le papier à photocopie
luh pahp•yay ah foh•toh•kuh•pee

129

Les Services

une agence de voyages oon ah•jahns duh vwah•yahj

CLUB de GYM

kluhb duh jeem

la piscine
lah pee•seen

LE PRESSING
NETTOYAGE À SEC

un nettoyage à sec
le pressing:
dry cleaner
une blanchisserie:
a laundry, they wash it!
une laverie libre-service:
(self-service) laundromat

le pressing
luh preh•seeng

LAVERIE LIBRE-SERVICE
lahv•ree lee•bruh sehr•vees

le linge
luh lehnj

une lessive
oon leh•seev

le lave-linge
luh lahv lehnj

le sèche-linge
luh sehsh lehnj

131

Les Services

Benjamin TAILLEUR
tah•yuhr

OPTICIEN
uhp•tees•yehn

les lunettes
lay loo•neht

les lunettes de soleil
lay loo•neht duh suh•leh•yuh

Fleuriste
fluh•reest

les fleurs
lay fluhr

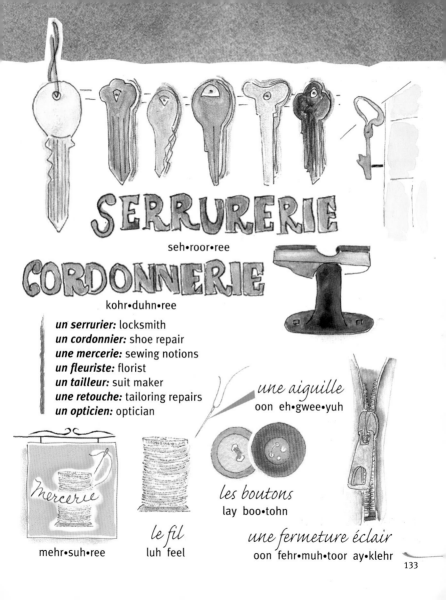

SERRURERIE
seh•roor•ree

CORDONNERIE
kohr•duhn•ree

un serrurier: locksmith
un cordonnier: shoe repair
une mercerie: sewing notions
un fleuriste: florist
un tailleur: suit maker
une retouche: tailoring repairs
un opticien: optician

une aiguille
oon eh•gwee•yuh

mercerie
mehr•suh•ree

le fil
luh feel

les boutons
lay boo•tohn

une fermeture éclair
oon fehr•muh•toor ay•klehr

133

salon de coiffure
sah•lohn duh kwah•foor

institut de beauté: beauty services for both men and women; facials, massage, etc.

salon de coiffure: hairdresser for both men and women

un rasage
uhn rah•zahj

le coiffeur
luh kwah•fuhr

une coupe
oon koop

un brushing: a wash and blow-dry

le séchoir
luh say•shwahr

un shampooing
uhn shahm•pwehn

Chez Le Coiffeur

une créme
oon krehm

une créme:
a conditioner and
usually very
expensive,
best to say
"pas de
créme"

une retouche
oon ruh•toosh

le rinçage
luh rehn•sahj

un balayage:
the French
way of
creating
highlights
by combing
in the color.
balayer: to
sweep

un balayage
uhn bah•leh•yahj

About tipping: Tips are
always included in the price;
something additional is always
appreciated.

une pédicure
oon pay•dee•koor

la laque
lah lahk

une manucure
oon mah•noo•koor

135

La Pharmacie

fahr•mah•see

Always look for the green cross.

l'huile solaire
lweel suh•lehr

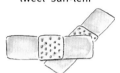

le médicament
luh may•dee•kah•mahn

l'aspirine
lahs•pee•reen

Emergency:
With an empty medicine bottle or a copy of your prescription, you can usually get it replaced.

les pansements
lay pahns•mahn

le préservatif
luh pray•zehr•vah•teef

un tampon
uhn tahm•pohn

les Kleenex
lay klee•nehks

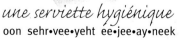

une serviette hygiénique
oon sehr•vee•yeht ee•jee•ay•neek

une solution pour lentilles
oon suh•loos•yohn poor lahn•tee•yuh

La Parapharmacie

un rouge à lèvres
uhn rooj ah leh•vruh

une pommade
oon puh•mahd

la parapharmacie: section within the *pharmacie* selling beauty products—herbal medicines and veterinarian products also found here.

un dissolvant
uhn dee•suhl•vahn

un mascara
uhn mahs•kah•rah

une parfumerie: sells perfume and name-brand cosmetics.

l'eau de cologne
loh duh kuh•luhn•yuh

le désodorisant
luh day•zoh•doh•ree•zahn

le talc
luh tahlk

une crème
oon krehm

137

L'Heure

le matin luh mah•tehn

1 a.m. = une heure (1h)
2 a.m. = deux heures (2h)
3 a.m. = trois heures (3h)
4 a.m. = quatre heures (4h)
5 a.m. = cinq heures (5h)
6 a.m. = six heures (6h)
7 a.m. = sept heures (7h)
8 a.m. = huit heures (8h)
9 a.m. = neuf heures (9h)
10 a.m. = dix heures (10h)
11 a.m. = onze heures (11h)
12 a.m. = douze heures (12h)

l'après-midi lah•preh•mee•dee

1 p.m. = treize heures (13h)
2 p.m. = quatorze heures (14h)
3 p.m. = quinze heures (15h)
4 p.m. = seize heures (16h)
5 p.m. = dix-sept heures (17h)
6 p.m. = dix-huit heures (18h)

le soir luh swahr

7 p.m. = dix-neuf heures (19h)
8 p.m. = vingt heures (20h)
9 p.m. = vingt et une heures (21h)
10 p.m. = vingt-deux heures (22h)
11 p.m. = vingt-trois heures (23h)
12 p.m. = minuit (24h)

about time:
h=the hour of

    19h
   −12
  = 7 p.m.

or simply say:
*sept heures
du soir.*

138

sept heures . . . (7h)
seht uhr

. . . quinze (7h 15)
kehnz

. . . trente (7h 30)
trahnt

. . . quarante-cinq (7h 45)
kah•rahnt sehnk

The French use the 24-hour clock, especially for store hours, entertainment, and transportation schedules.

Note: *24h/24h* indicates a shop is open around the clock.

Pronunciation of numbers, p. 118

le jour
luh joor

la nuit
lah nwee

une montre
oon mohn•truh

une horloge
oon uhr•luhj

midi (12h)
mee•dee

minuit (24h)
mee•nwee

Le Calendrier

le calendrier
luh kah•lahn•dree•yay

les jours
lay joor

dimanche dee•mahn•shuh
lundi luhn•dee
mardi mahr•dee
mercredi mehr•kruh•dee
jeudi juh•dee
vendredi vahn•druh•dee
samedi sahm•dee

JANVIER

		1	2	3	4	5
6	7	8	9	10	11	12
13	14	15	16	17	18	19
20	21	22	23	24	25	26
27	28	29	30	31		

le mois
luh mwah

les années
layz ah•nay

une semaine
oon suh•meh•nuh

January 8, 2002
Note:
the day comes first.

8 / 01 / 2002
day month year

2000 = *deux mille*
duh meel

2001 = *deux mille un*
duh meel uhn

2002 = *deux mille deux*
duh meel duh

Les Mois   Les Saisons

l'hiver
lee•vehr

décembre
day•sahm•bruh

janvier
jahn•vee•yay

février
fay•vree•yay

le printemps
luh prehn•tahn

mars
mahrs

avril
ah•vreel

mai
may

l'automne
loh•tuh•nuh

septembre
sehp•tahm•bruh

octobre
uhk•tuh•bruh

novembre
nuh•vahm•bruh

l'été
lay•tay

juin
jwehn

juillet
jwee•yeh

août
oot

Le Temps

le brouillard
luh broo•yahr

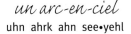

les nuages
lay noo•wahj

un arc-en-ciel
uhn ahrk ahn see•yehl

la pluie
lah plwee

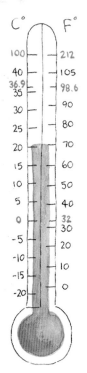

C°	F°
100	212
40	105
36.9	98.6
35	90
30	80
25	70
20	60
15	50
10	40
5	32
0	30
-5	20
-10	10
-15	0
-20	

Celsius
sehl•see•yoos

convert
Celsius
to Fahrenheit

$$20°C$$
$$\times 2$$
$$40$$
$$+\ 32$$
$$72°F$$

Fahrenheit
fah•ren•ite

convert
Fahrenheit
to Celsius

$$72°F$$
$$-32$$
$$2\overline{)40}$$
$$20°C$$

la température
lah tahm•pay•rah•toor

le soleil
luh suh•leh•yuh

142

Les Toilettes

1. **une Sanisette**
   oon sah•nee•zeht

Les toilettes:

1. On the street: look for *une Sanisette* (a small charge).

2. At a café: buy a coffee or water at the bar if you're uncomfortable just using the facilities. *Les toilettes* and telephones are most often downstairs, *au sous-sol*. Often in *les toilettes*, the light doesn't go on until you lock the door. Don't panic!

3. In the *métro*

4. Or, look for this sign.

   . . . and there are always train stations, department stores, and hotels.

4. You always ask for *"les toilettes,"* not *la toilette.*
   lay twah•leht

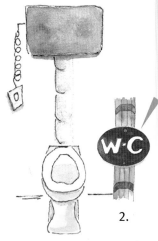

2.

un W.-C. (water closet)
uhn doo•bluh•vay say

3.

Au Secours!

oh suh•koor

une ambulance
oon ahm•boo•lahns

urgence médicale
oor•jahns may•dee•kahl

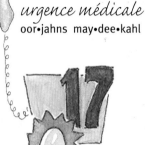

un docteur
uhn duhk•tuhr

Au secours: HELP!

Dial 18 for the ambulance as well as the fire department.

Dial 15 for the doctor and 17 for the police.

le policier
luh puh•lees•yay

une voiture de police
oon vwah•toor duh puh•lees

les pompiers
lay pohmp•yay

une voiture de pompiers
oon vwah•toor duh pohmp•yay

— *u* —

— *v* —

— *w* —

— *xyz* —

When in doubt, spell it out

a	ah	n	ehn
b	bay	o	oh
c	cay	p	pay
d	day	q	koo
e	uh	r	ehr
f	ehf	s	ehs
g	jay	t	tay
h	ahsh	u	oo
i	ee	v	vay
j	jee	w	doo•bluh•vay
k	kah	x	eeks
l	ehl	y	ee•grehk
m	ehm	z	zehd